HOW TO TIME YOUR SEWING MACHINE

OR

HOW TO MAKE SURE YOUR WIFE
WILL STAY WITH YOU
FOREVER!

BY

Mike Riley

Published and Printed
By Mike Riley
Aboard the Ketch Beau Soleil
Somewhere on the Seven Seas

sailingbooks@rocketmail.com

ISBN   978-0-9828247-6-4

This Book is dedicated to Karen, my wife,
who has been sewing all her life.
She can sew such a straight seam.
She is a Sea Captain's dream
come true.
Karen, I love you.

I really do! Honest! Her ability to sew is just a bonus!
Course, she has other bonuses, too!

Table of Contents

Conclusion

Introduction

Hello fellow adventurer, sailor and sailmaker, my name is Mike Riley and together with my wife, Karen, we are on our third true circumnavigation of the world. (To be true, a circumnavigation must be completed on the same boat, you must anchor as close as possible to the exact spot you departed from, (none of this crossing the outward wake stuff) and you have to have a really, truly, seriously great party on the day you finish. I know you are tired and in no mood for a party, but the rules, you will find, are different for circumnavigators. People will expect more from you.)

We have ripped a lot of sails during our voyages which we repaired ourselves using our faithful little sewing machine designed for home use. Needless to say it often got out of whack (to use a technical term) and needed to be re-timed. After awhile, unfortunately, I became proficient at it and here for the first time ever in print, are Mike Riley's tricks on how to time your sewing Machine.

Throughout this book I refer to sewing machines as 'The Machine' partially in respect to the great men who created it: Walter Hunt of New York City, in 1832, the true creator who never patented it; Elias Howe of Spencer, Mass. In 1846, who came up with the same idea, (independently, as they say), fourteen years later and Isaac Merrit Singer, Pittstown, N.Y. in 1851 who invented the overhanging arm. In order that more people could buy his machines, Singer also invented installment credit plans and so is partially to blame for the world's present financial difficulties! Also I refer to the Machine to try to share some respect for the weight of a sewing machine. It is heavy. Don't let it fall on your toe. Really. It hurts. I should know. It is why I had to figure out how to time Machines in the first place! And I don't even want to talk about the time 'the Machine' sank the dinghy.

It isn't difficult to time any sewing Machine. All of them work on the same principles, with slight differences, none of which are hard to understand. Besides, would you go to sea without knowing how to fix your engine? Really, you should also know how to repair the major propulsion unit of your vessel, your sails; and to know how to keep the tool to fix them, running.

Don't feel you have to read this book, cover to cover. Open the book to the chapter describing the problem you are facing. Study the diagrams. Locate all the parts described before altering anything. If you are good at fixing outboards, sewing machines will present no difficulties. If not, it would be a good idea to take digital photos of each step as you proceed so that if need be you can return 'the Machine' to the pre-repair state. When tightening or loosening a bolt, it is always a good idea to count the turns you make unless you have a good understanding and feeling for torque.

The ultimate test for the success of the timing will be how well the Machine sews. Feel free to alter a setting, then before altering another, have a little test sew. Always test on the material you intend to sew on later.

Sewing and sailmaking are traditional blue water arts. When people ask who repaired the sails, you should stand tall, look 'em straight in the eye, and tell 'em, "I did." After all you are a sailor, not a yachtsman, or you wouldn't be reading this book in the first place. One day, if you keep the water on the outside, the mast pointed up, and the sails maintained, you will complete your circle of the world. On that day, be sure to remember your little sewing Machine, it helped you make it around the globe.

My wife, Karen says not everyone wants to go around the world, but that can't be. It is so much fun, playing James T. Kirk, or is that Captain Cook? I always get them mixed up! Anyway, half the fun of boats is fixing them up, then taking them to sea to practice your steely, captain look. Anyway, around the world or around the bay, you should have your sewing machine ready to go.

Cleaning

Advanced Players May Skip This Section

Do you remember when your mother taught you that cleanliness is next to godliness? Guess what, Sailmaker, she was right. A sewing Machine is not going to work correctly if it is full of lint, cut off pieces of thread, stray pieces of material all oil saturated and stuck in the bearings and other moving parts. If you want your Machine to work properly, you have to keep it clean.

Commercially, sewing machine operators are required to stop work fifteen minutes before the whistle to clean their machine for the following day. I know you have just preformed a miracle of endurance by sewing non-stop for hours repairing your ripped jib and finally you have finished the damn thing and now I telling you that you have to clean up the mess? What next, am I'm going to tie you to the grate and pull the cat out of its bag? How can you get off this hell ship?

OK, I'll give you a break. Clean your Machine later. After all the Captain wants you to go and raise the damn sail now anyway, the slave driver. But don't forget. Tie a string around your finger, leave yourself a message, put a lipstick note on the Captain's forehead when he is asleep. But don't forget. Don't forget. The thing is, living in a saltwater environment like we do and sewing salt impregnated sails, the oils and lint in our Machine are salt and oil saturated. It was bad enough with nice little pieces of thread strangling our bearings, but now they are loaded with grainy, sharp edged, corrosive salt turning our expensive Machine into a rusted out hulk. With practice it isn't hard to clean your Machine and it is a good way to introduce some of the moving parts. So get out a little screwdriver, a half inch artist's paint brush, tweezers, cleaning fluid, a magnifying glass, and a mop (just kidding) and lets do some cleaning!

The Needle

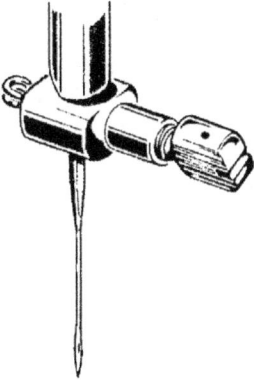

So your needle doesn't need cleaning? It is already nice and shiny? Is that so? Take out your magnifying glass. There is a thumb screw on the needle bar. Turn it to the left to release the needle. On sewing machines it is always left to loosen, right to tighten. Don't drop the needle. The first thing you will notice is the needle is not at all like a regular sewing needle. The eye is at the pointy end and the needle is not uniformly round. One side is either flat or has a groove carved into its side. Inspect the tip. Needles only last on the average of fifteen hours of continual use. The slightest little burr on the tip will make your machine miss the occasional stitch and make the tension erratic, and make your painstaking sewing job look sloppy. Inspect the needle for the slightest sign of rust or the mildest of bends or burrs. Both will result in a poor looking sewing job. If there are mild imperfections grab a piece of 1200 grit sand paper and touch up the needle.

Eventually you will have to buy more needles. There, there, it is OK. Stop crying. The Captain will pay for it. They are not expensive. Think of all the money you're saving by doing the job yourself. At the store, don't freak out when they ask you what kind, you will find that there are four different types of needles:

1. Sharps. Alright, alright. You already knew that needles are sharp. I got that. At least they didn't name them X2nw9. Sharps are the needles we will use most often in making clothes, awnings and sails. They are designed to penetrate the sailcloth without undo damage.

2. Ball Points. These guys have a rounded point to enable them to go around the threads of the cloth rather than penetrate into the cloth's threads. They are made for soft cloth, not the armor plated material sails are made of.

3. Wedge Points. These are a little like hand sail needles. They are sword like and cut open a hole in the material for the sewing machine's threads to go. They aren't good for sewing sails with sewing machines. They tend to make the sail material run. But will work fine for the leather around the clew and foot.

4. Metallic. Don't worry about these. They are made for metallic threads. They won't work for sail repair or awnings. But don't buy them by mistake, either.

All needles have little numbers inscribed on the sides telling you what size the needle is. The heavier the material you are working on, the heavier the needle has to be. We don't have to worry about the needle choice except when we go to the store to buy new ones. On boats we only use sharps, normally. The above needle choices are just to make sure you buy the right one for sail repair. If you decide to branch out into other endeavors, get the right needle for the job.

The Top Tension Discs

These are underneath the little dial thing just above and slightly to the left on the front of the Machine. The front of the Machine is the side with all the controls! The top thread goes through these discs which tighten and loosen as the demands of the Machine dictate. (Remember the Machine is spelled always in capital letters. You are but a vestal virgin and/or altar boy serving the commands of the Machine. If the Machines demands are not met, you will be back to repairing sails by hand. Not a good idea. Don't think of the Machine as a tool. It is your personal god! Worship it! Keep it covered when you are not honoring it to keep dust away. Offer it only the best of machine oils. Keep it spotless and clean!)

You are going to spend a lot of your sewing time, adjusting the top tension. You might as well become familiar with it. Take a piece of cloth with some sewing Machine oil on it. Run it back and forth between the discs while the tension is at its weakest setting. (Turn the dial to the left to open, to lessen the tension, to the right to increase the tension.) Then do it again with a dry cloth (old tee shirts work well) to make sure there aren't any threads stuck in there and to wipe out any excess oil.

The Motor and Belt

Clean the motor? Hate to tell you sailmaker, but on a big sail those pesky little threads get everywhere. Electric motors have cooling vents in the outside casing. Get into the habit of making sure there are no threads sucked into the casing. The threads are non conductive, they won't shock you, but they will ruin the bearings and make the motor run slower. Pull the threads out with your tweezers, with the electric plug out of its socket, please. (Unless you have always wanted curly hair.) We are going to need all the power we need. Keep your motor clean.

Never oil the belt. Ever. It won't help. All it will do is make the rubber deteriorate faster. If the belt is slipping under load, tighten it by adjusting the distance the motor is away from the hand wheel. The frame of the motor has two screws in slots (or one in a slot and one in a hole) holding the motor to the house of the Machine. Loosen the screws, tighten the belt and secure the motor again. Some belts work better with the points on one side of the belt facing out. It is kind of a Zen thing!

The Black Hole of Calcutta

You know about the Black Hole, don't you? It is the place in India which once you enter, all hope is abandoned. You did know that your sewing Machine had a black hole, didn't you? It is below the needle, under the needle plate, down where strange equipment twirls in arcs and it is the place where dead threads go to die and then to haunt untidy seamstressers.

I'm sorry to have to tell you, Sailmaker, but you are going to be spending a lot of time in the black hole. However, with courage, foresight, tweezers, an oil can, a good flashlight and a crucifix, there is no reason you can't make it back up again to the light of day.

There are two safe ways to access the Black Hole. One, for adventurous souls only, is to slide back the throat plate and slide plate and/or the needle plate (the shiny metal plates through which the needle projects while sewing). To make it easier, remove the presser foot (the foot shaped thing that the needle goes through and that goes up and down to allow the material being sewn to be adjusted. It has a knurled knob holding it in place. (Turn left to loosen, right to tighten) Otherwise, you have no doubt noticed that the Machine is mounted on hinges. You can lift the front of the Machine up and expose the Black Hole to the light of day.

Either way you proceed, you are looking at a once closely guarded secret back in the 1800's, the secret of the sewing machine. If you have been sewing for awhile and only opened this book because your Machine has stopped working, there will be plenty of lint, threads, strings and who knows what other weird stuff the aliens snuck in when you weren't looking, in and around the Black Hole. If you swung the Machine up on it's hinges you will be seeing two sections of the bottom of the machine. The Black Hole proper is the side on the left, the needle

16

Alignment "Prick"

Bottom Tension Tab

Bobbin Case

Bobbin

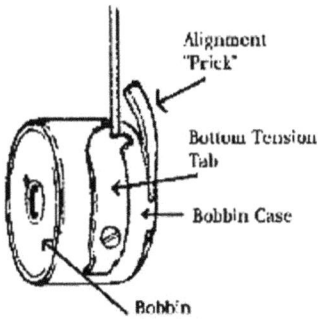

side, not the wheel side. The wheel side is the Pit of Despair. (Just Kidding!)

As you clean up the Black Hole (I don't have to tell you that you HAVE to clean up after the Machine every chance you get, do I? My wife, Karen, once worked at a loft where the sailmakers could make as much mess as they wanted, they could even throw stuff on the floor, after hours, the men had to come and clean up their Machines. I think she would have worked there for free, she really enjoyed the idea of them cleaning up her mess, slaving at her feet.)

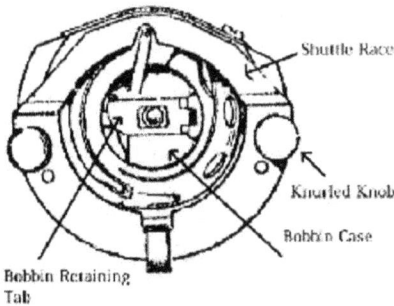

Shuttle Race

Knurled Knob

Bobbin Case

Bobbin Retaining Tab

As you clean up the Black Hole notice the weird contraption under the needle. I shouldn't say contraption, it is the invention that started the industrial revolution. This is what you are seeing. The two knurled knobs on either side that twist open, twist left to open, then push or pull to the side. Don't do it yet! Really! As soon as you do the whole thing is going to fall out into your (hopefully) waiting hands. The outside is the race. The race in the Machine is the thing that keeps the horses running around in a circle. If it wasn't for the race the horses would run off in all directions, ignoring stoplights, scaring

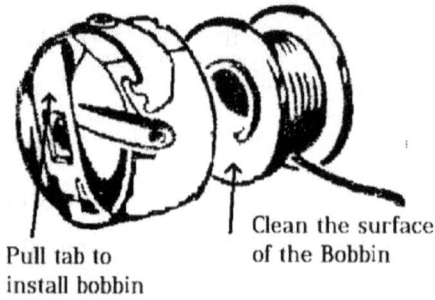

Pull tab to install bobbin

Clean the surface of the Bobbin

kids, twisting the thread all up and no sails would ever be made. The bobbin case has a little prick looking thing (we are all adults here, aren't we?) that fits into a little (OK, I'll clean it up) slot on the top of the race. Be sure to remember that when re-installing the shuttle race. Isn't this just so exciting?! I mean, WOW! The excitement is just too much to handle!

OK, you twist the knobs and force them to the sides and the whole kit and caboodle falls into your hands. (Did I say that whenever you are working in the Black Hole the needle has to be withdrawn to its highest height?) (No? Well, if you didn't, when the whole kit and caboodle fell into your hands, it also bent your needle. Bummer, huh?) In your hands lie the shuttle race, the shuttle, the bobbin case and the bobbin.

It doesn't get much better than this, hey! For some reason (known only to aliens) this association of mechanical ingenuity (and who says I don't know any big words?) that you are holding in your hands likes, hell, loves, to collect threads, lint, scraps of last week's material, salt, old oil, your lunch and anything else you are missing. Everytime you clean your machine, you are going to have to clean the Black Hole, so get friendly with it. Love it. (Hey, stop with the faces, I didn't say 'make' and 'to', did I?) What a tough crowd!

Because of the salt in our sea going world, we have to be on the alert for rust. The bobbin is one of the worse culprits. Everytime you clean the Black Hole check every surface for the slightest sign of discoloration. If you see some polish it out with some 2000 grit sand paper. Some people like to squirt WD-40 all over their Machine. Don't do it. Sure it is easy and all, but it is also a much lower quality of oil than machine oil. When you consider the tiny amount of oil you are going to use each week, do your Machine a favor, stay with the good stuff. (I mean they sell WD-40 for a dollar or two on sale! You get what you pay for.

The Foot Pedal

Some people say that the foot pedal was put on earth to torture poor souls so the descent into hell won't be as big a shock. They aren't all wrong. The foot pedal does have considerable voltage and amperage running through it, and if it isn't in perfectly perfect working condition it can give you a nasty shock. And your Captain Bligh expects you to sew straight seams while the Machine is sending waves of pain through your body?

So, don't forget, while cleaning your Machine to remember to clean the foot pedal. After all, it is down there on the floor where all the stray pieces of material and threads eventually end up. All it takes is a couple of threads and you have a short circuit. I don't have to tell you when it will happen. Believe me, you will know it!

HINT! Pull the plug out of the wall, turn off your inverter, stop the generator. Never, never approach the foot pedal especially with the left hand. (The heart is on the left side.) There are no capacitors in a sewing Machine, however it is always a good idea to wait a few minutes to let any stray pulses of electrons to die off before servicing the foot pedal. If you think I am trying to scare the living daylights out of you, you are right. However there is no danger if you proceed in a proper manner. In fact, on second thought, I think you should make the Captain do it! Everyone knows they have tough skin.

Often there are cooling vents in the foot pedal and this is where the threads most often sneak into. If you have a vacuum cleaner an easier way to clean the pedal is to suck out any material with the hose. If not, then you are back to tweezers and a flashlight like the rest of us!

How It is Supposed to Work

Sorry, before you can time your machine, you really should have an idea of how a stitch is made or you will just be blindly following instructions and at the end will still not have the vaguest idea of what went wrong. So with out further ado, let's pull out our tools and dissect our little machine. Open her up! Involuntary surgery! Heh, heh, heh. Say it really loud. I'll bet that machine will fix itself, out of pure fear!

The needle is not like a hand sewing needle. First of all the eye is on the opposite end and just above the eye is either a flat space or a slot where the thread hides as the needle goes into the material. If it couldn't hide, the friction of going through the material would really, really throw the timing off. When the needle has gone down as far as it can, it starts back up but leaves a loop of thread because the take up arm (we will cover this stuff later) is now on its downward path and there is no tension on the upper thread. Just as the needle goes up, the shuttle hook that half oscillates around the bobbin picks up the loop of top thread and pulls it around the bottom thread coming from the bobbin. The shuttle doesn't go around in a circle, just back and forth in a semi arc. As the

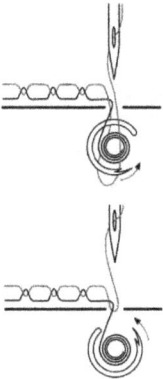

needle pulls up, the feed dogs come up and moves the material along to get it ready for the next stitch.

That wasn't so hard, was it? Your hair is falling out? You are using your magnifying glass to hammer this book? Don't worry. Keep reading. It is ok to scream and yell. I think it helps sometimes. Of course I might have left out a few minor items but we will get to them in time. Now, now. Calm yourself. It is going to be alright. Try breathing deeply.

In sewing machines timing is everything. Everything has to happen just at the right time. If the shuttle hook turns too soon or too late there will be no stitch. If the needle pulls out too early or late, there will be no stitch. There are many ways the process can get out timing but the one that fails most often is the distance the needle goes down into the material. Either it doesn't go far enough and the thread doesn't form the right loop or it goes too far and the needle hits the shuttle and gets bent. OK, lets time the needle first.

Basic Tricky Operating Tips

Everyone knows how to sew. It says that right there on the showroom sign, just after, Yours for only $19.95 a month. But don't believe it. It takes years to be able to sew really well. Luckily we don't have to perform miracles of seamstress-ry. We just have to repair our sails, make new sail covers, build an awning, and make a few nifty doo-dads for the boat. (Gulp!) To be able to do that will only take an afternoon of reading—and this isn't even a long book! Before we can time your machine, lets make sure you are not going to whack it out of timing again the next time you touch it. OK? Alright. It is easy to sew, just takes a little info, a little practice and there you are! A modern day miracle worker!

1. Always, always be sure the machine is correctly threaded and the bobbin lint free before beginning any project. The bobbin hides down there in the Black Hole of Calcutta where all demons dwell. Never fear. If you have to, shine your brightest flash light right in their eyes, looking for dirt and lint. Demons hate that.
2. Use the right needle. If you have any domestic machine, the needle will be the same length. Sail-Rites use a

slightly longer needle. The heavier the material the thicker the needle will have to be. Needles come with their widths inscribed on the top part of the needle on the shank. First comes a metric number, a forward slash and then an arbitrary number the heaviest being 20, the lightest, 8. (Don't ask why. It is something the aliens told us to do.) For example, for fine silk, you would use a #60/8. For very heavy sailcloth, #120/19. Don't use a heavier needle than needed or you will end up with yucky big holes in your material. Make sure the thread goes through the eye easily, or it will mess up your timing.

3. Use the right type of needle. The needle you want is a sharp. Hey, I know they are all sharp. But that is what they called it, OK. The next closest is a ball point which, naturally, is less sharp, better for knits, etc. Just to confuse the poor sailor, they combine different types of needles. So you can buy a slightly ball point sharp. If I knew I had to be this smart in life, I would have stayed in school longer! There are also metallic thread needles, serger needles, wedge points, to name just a few not to be fooled into buying. Needles only last ten to twenty hours. Get used to buying them. Get sharps.

4. Use exactly the same thread in the bobbin as the top thread. When filling the bobbin, don't fill it too high. Usually your machine will automatically stop winding. If it doesn't, less is more. If the thread falls off the bobbin

down there in the 'Black Hole of Calcutta' it is going to make a big mess and will probably bend your needle.

5. Always pull the bobbin thread up thru the base plate before starting to sew (turning the hand wheel towards you while holding on to the top thread will bring the bottom thread up from the Black Hole) . Always pull the bobbin and top threads to the back of the machine before starting to sew and hold them tight past and under the presser foot as you make your first stitch.

6. To jump start the motor turn the hand wheel towards you. As the needle starts to dull, you will have to do this more often. Don't ever turn the top of the wheel away from you, even while sewing in reverse.

7. Always start and stop your machine with the needle and slack thread take up lever in the up position. Only when you are turning the fabric should you leave the needle in the fabric. (Raising the presser foot, turning the material, and lowering the foot again.) It is very easy to bend your needle while twisting and turning a big sail. Consider stopping your seam and then starting again if you have a huge rolled up sail under your Machine's arm.

8. Once you have finally got the tension adjusted correctly, both top and bobbin tension, just change the top tension for little changes. I will talk a lot more about tension, next. But as a general rule never change the bobbin tension if you don't really have to. If you use your machine for sail repair and fixing clothes, get another

bobbin for the lighter work. Don't worry if you are saying, 'What is he talking about?' We are going to talk a LOT about tension. (Thank goodness!)

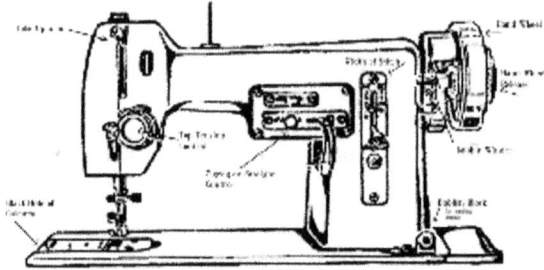

9. Always cover your machine while not using it. Have you looked at your National Geographics when they talk about Troy? It is buried under tons of dirt. Seen how many feet of dirt have fallen on the Earth in three millennium? Some people think all this dirt is micro asteroids from space, others think it is jetsam from UFO's. And we wonder where all these new diseases come from, no doubt from UFO's holding tanks. Well, where else are they going to dump it? In any case, we don't want any dirt falling on our machines.

10. Know your Machine. You should know a lot more about your machine than you know about your loved ones. Not that the damn thing isn't as frustrating as a loved one can be, but hey, after all it is just a Machine, isn't it?

Tension

Let's talk about tension. The Machine's tension, not the screaming fits you have when that devil spawn Machine refuses to operate. Every time you sit down at your sewing machine from now till kingdom come, you are going to have to adjust your tension. So you might as well get used to it. You might as well be able to adjust it with total confidence. If you are tense while adjusting your tension, take a break. If your significant other

asks why you aren't fixing the sail, tell him to light candles, burn some incense, put on some smoothing music. Never adjust your Machine's tension until you are at peace with yourself! It does help to breathe deeply while adjusting tension. It does help to go out on the foredeck and release a primal scream that will placate the Tension gods. Those yogis would have been great sailmakers!

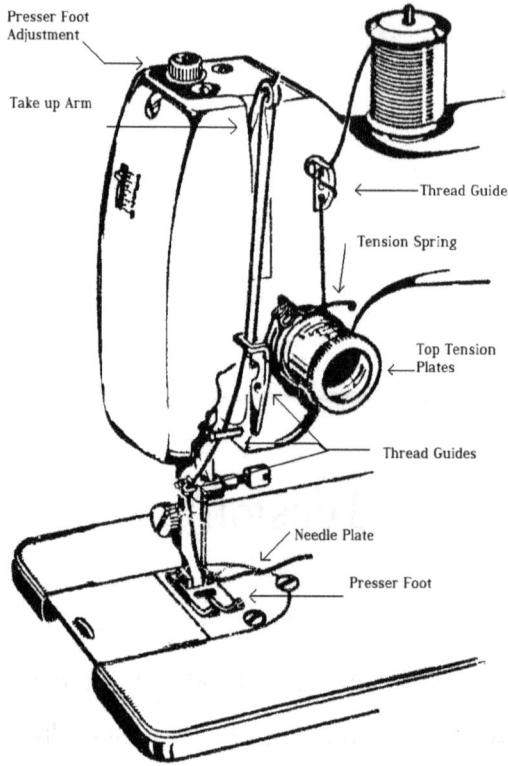

Presser Foot
Adjustment

Take up Arm

Thread Guide

Tension Spring

Top Tension
Plates

Thread Guides

Needle Plate

Presser Foot

To make a perfect stitch both the top and bottom tensions must be in total harmony, chanting some of that Zen stuff together! Normally, unless your Machine is totally, completely, screwed up, just adjust the top tension to achieve 'total' harmony.

There are two discs that the top thread goes between during its threading process. As you tighten or loosen (right to tighten, left to loosen) the dial between these two discs the tension of the thread at the needle will change.

The top thread goes thru a maze of holes and gates in the threading process. Your book that came with the machine will tell you exactly how the thread must be strung. If you miss or go the wrong way thru a gate, your machine has no hope of working.

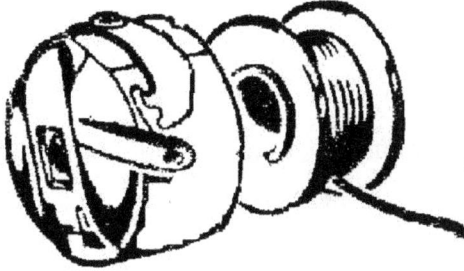

Bobbin and Bobbin Case

If directions didn't come with your machine, look on the internet. If you can't find your machine on the internet, the process is usually very logical.

Start from the top of the machine, go thru a block (I'm a sailor, OK!), or guide, just above the tension discs, go between the discs and under a little spring hook thingy (that is an important technical term!), hence to the Take Up Arm. Do this when the arm is at its highest point thus raising the needle up high too, (turn the wheel to make it move) then down thru a series of blocks (don't miss any) to the needle. The last block before the needle is most important. It is always on the same side as the flat side or grooved side of the needle. (Needle section coming up!)

If, after diligent attempts to correct the tension by changing the top tension, then and only then adjust the bottom tension. When bottom tension is too tight it will result in broken threads and bent needles. When bottom tension is too loose you will create a bird nest of thread under the presser foot in the Black Hole of Calcutta that will seriously screw up your timing and most likely bend your needle.

The bottom thread starts out on the bobbin. The bobbin goes into the bobbin case. The bobbin case has a slit for the thread to come out. To insert the bobbin pull out the little lever on the outside of the case. This also locks the bobbin inside the case. Insert the bobbin so the thread is wound up clockwise as you look at the bobbin. (Karen says different machines have their bobbins threads go in differently, but every machine I have ever worked on, worked better with the bobbin thread wound so it comes out of the bobbin case as you look at it from the bobbin side, right to left. I think this is just another way to increase tension. The bobbin case has one or two screws for adjusting the little flange where the thread exits the case. (Right to tighten, left to loosen). An sixteenth of a turn makes a lot of difference. If there are two screws, adjust the one away from the thread exit, its right to loosen, left to tighten. The tension should be set at first so there is just a slight but noticeable drag of the thread. Never, never, NEVER run your machine without any drag on the thread coming out of the bobbin case.

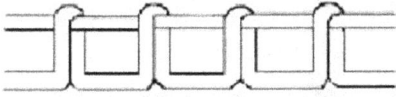

To test the tension it is sometimes useful to put a different color, but same type and weight, thread in the bobbin to see where the problem is. If the bottom color is being pulled to the top during a test sew, then the top tension is too tight, or the bottom tension is too loose. Always assume the bottom tension is correct and try to adjust the top tension first. If the top color is being pulled to the bottom of the material then tighten the top tension.

Below is an example of top tension being too tight. The top thread is pulled tight forcing the bottom thread to come up and loop over it before returning to the bottom. This allows the materials to slide back and forth as they are not sufficiently pinioned.

Turn the page upside down and you can see what a stitch looks like with the bottom tension too tight. If the stitch is correct, you will see only the top threads color on top, only the bottom threads color on the bottom and the connection is buried

31

in the material itself, far, far away from the sun, chafe, stays and masts while tacking.

Now, if the knots are buried, only two things can be wrong. If the material is puckering, both tensions are too tight. Loosen the bottom tension first and adjust the top tension to match. If the stitches are too loose, not holding the material tightly, both tensions are too loose. Tighten the bottom tension first.

There that wasn't too bad was it? Hey, stop swearing and throwing stuff! Once the machine is set up properly, it really tends to stay that way. If after all the above has been tried and the machine still refuses to work even during a dark night in the middle of a thunder storm, then your machine has to be timed. It is out of whack, to use a technical term. So turn the page and…

Timing the Needle Bar and Shuttle Hook

Or- 99 times out of a hundred it is the damn needle bar.

The needle is attached to a shaft that goes up and down, plunging and withdrawing the needle into the material where it not only guides the top thread into the stitch but also presents the top thread to the shuttle where the knot is formed with the lower thread. The depth that the needle descends into the material is of utmost importance in the sewing process. It is not difficult to adjust. What we are going to do is adjust the timing between the needle and the shuttle hook. Ready? You aren't? You are confused? OK, I'll try again.

Sewing machines are created to make knots. That is what they do best. Sewing machines can make knots faster than any Boy Scout that ever lived. Plus they make a series of knots that connect two or more layers of cloth. To make a knot, the Machine bends, twists, twirls, the bottom and top threads together. It does this by looping the top thread around the bottom thread. It does that by looping the top thread around the bobbin where the bottom thread is coming out of. Better? No? Arrrggggg!

Remember when you were a lifeguard (or were in love/lust with one, and he/she had to lace a series of knots in the line that was connected to the life ring. When he/she threw it, the line magically unknotted as it flew over the pool. The sewing machine makes the same kind of knot. Remember when you pulled that thread on your favorite sweater and it fell to pieces? That is what sewing machines do to your sails. Scary, huh! Just like it took you hours to learn how to tie that knot while the lifeguard was watching (the chills!) it will take a bit of time to figure out a sewing machine. So keep reading. All will become clearer.

Turn the machine, upright, needle end towards you, wheel away from you. Just above the needle bar, the shaft that the needle is attached to, is an opening inspection cover. Sometimes it is opened by turning a large screw, sometimes by a serrated twist knob. The cover always opens right to left, towards the

34

back of the machine or comes off in one piece. The screw opens counterclockwise. Ready? Open the cover.

OK. Stop screaming. You can figure it out. It is only a machine. It is not a Terminator. Have I told you the power should be off? Turn off the power. Unplug the machine. Always turn off the power before dealing with alien intelligences. Just kidding! Right in the middle of the exposed gear case is the needle bar. If you have a Singer, the bar will be marked with two horizontal lines (sideways) 3/32" (2.4mm) apart. Don't get upset about the 3/32". (three thirty two seconds of an inch). It is just like a eighth of an inch only a bit smaller. I think Hunt, Howe and Singer, the guys who invented and refined the sewing machine had a thing for 3/32". Maybe it is an inventor thing. Just so you have a feeling for the measurement, 1/32" is just ever so slightly over the width of a cheap cd.

Turn the hand wheel, always turn the top towards you, towards the front of the machine, until the needle is at it's lowest position. (If there is no thread in the needle you can turn the hand wheel either way). At this point the top thread that the needle has pulled down under the material is still tight to the needle but as the needle starts back up, the top thread will start to make a loop next to the needle that soon will be picked up by the shuttle hook.

OK, I know you are confused. What is happening is the Machine is being very tricky. As it lowers the needle it is releasing the top tension, (the discs are slightly separating) lowering the take up bar, (the fishing pole thing that sticks out in front of the machine and goes up and down like it is jigging for fish) at the same time the shuttle hook (we will get to this in a minute) down in the black hole is getting ready to grab the top thread and have its way with it. (No, no, no. Believe it or not, the bottom thread, bobbin, shuttle, shuttle race, shuttle hook, and foot cause fewer problems than the beautiful top thread that you can always keep your eye on. Isn't that the way. It is always the goody two shoes that cause the biggest problems!) (OK. Not true. Those bad terrorists made me write that.)

The needle is all the way down. It is down as far as it is going to go. It is almost ready to go back up. The top tension is starting to tighten but the take up bar is still going down, so there is no strain on the top thread. We need to measure how far down the needle is at this point but we will do that later. Right now we are just doing an overview, a flyby, a glimpse at the GPS before charging on thru the break in the reef, a last glance at the heavens before going off the high board, a final wrenching of the gut before…

Back on the subject, the needle starts to go back up and the friction of the material being sewn thru prevents the top thread from following the needle up. The top thread is abandoned down there in the black hole, the poor thing, and it is forced to form a loop out of its excess thread, it is circling the wagons against demons when the shuttle hook (more on this later) comes racing in, roughly grabs the poor top thread and drags it around in a half of a circle before it gets bored of our very polite top thread and lets it go. Just as the hook lets the top thread go, the take up bar (the fishing pole thing) quickly pulls up and the top thread is pulled out of the black hole to safety! Hurray!

While all this is happening the bottom thread is sitting there in its bobbin watching all this activity happen all around him. He is a good old boy, with a simple job. All he has to do is ease out the bottom thread at an even rate and not get dizzy while doing it. Of course, nothing in life is that easy. As he is easing out his thread, he is spun around and the Machine stops pulling his thread out. He isn't worried. He has his beer and peanuts and a rerun of the Michael Jordan led Bulls are on the TV. Nothing bothers the bobbin. Well, almost nothing. If you wind too much thread onto the bobbin, it is like giving him too much beer. He will upchuck it all out and make an unholy mess. Don't over feed him!

Just when the top thread is almost all the way out of the black hole, just in the middle of the material being sewn, she is abandoned. The take up arm stops taking up, the tension plates stop tensioning and the needle starts going down again with a new piece of top thread. But at that last second, that very last second when the bobbin is pulling, the top tension is still tensioning and the take up arm is still taking up, that is when timing is at its most important. In that very last second, just at that very last second, everybody gives a little tug that tightens the knot in the material being sewn and buries the knot deep in the material where it is nice and safe and away from the rough abrasive world or chafe and sunlight. If one guy pulls too soon or too late, the knot is messy, the stitch is ruined, the captain is livid, you are sent to the mast head without bread or water. Everybody has to pull together. Everyone has to be on the same team. They have to have their timing right.

While all this is happening the presser foot is advancing the material forward to ready for the next stitch, but lets ignore the next stitch for the moment. Lets look at just one stitch and how we should time it, and how to adjust it if it is out of whack.

In order for a knot to be made the needle and hook have to be timed to near perfection. (Perfection would be nice, but listen, as soon as we finish timing the machine we are going to be ramming the needle into all manners of materials until it gets ever so slightly out of timing again. So let's not get carried away. Get as close as you can and get back to sewing again. With practice, timing can be corrected on a machine you are familiar with in five minutes. (As long as you don't get carried away with ten ounce brand new, armor plated, sailcloth.)

Turn the hand wheel until the needle is at it's lowest point. Oh, yeah, you did that already! Are you sure? Make sure it is at it's lowest point. Continue the rotation until the needle has risen 3/32" (2.4mm). Stop. The shuttle hook is approaching the needle. The eye of the needle has to be just below the point of the hook as the point of the hook just reaches the needle. There it is going to pick up the loop of top thread, carry it around the bobbin, thus creating a knot. OK, road stop.

Aliens like to be confusing. That is why we haven't caught them yet at their evil designs. So, knowing their designs, it should be of no surprise that there are three hooks on the shuttle, and the hook (the one in the middle) that we have to measure is always hidden by the shuttle race. The shuttle race is the part that holds the whole alien contraption together. There has to be some anti gravity device in there that we haven't been smart enough to discover yet. It is held to the Machine by two knurled knobs (anti-slip devices common on alien space craft). Loosen the knobs, force them to the sides and the shuttle race, bobbin case and bobbin will fall off into your hand. Be quick. The shuttle will also try to fall off. Hold it in place. We need to measure its distance from the needle and its distance above the top of the eye of the needle. The thing is, there must be enough of a loop in the top thread for the shuttle hook to pick up EVERY SINGLE TIME. We don't want any missed stitches. The best way to do this is to raise the needle 3/32" from its lowest depths.

OK. The needle is raised 3/32". The point of the hook should now be a maximum of 3/32" above the eye of the needle or the width of 3 cd's.   At the minimum it should be one cd above the eye and that is pushing it. You want the maximum loop the needle can give you so the shuttle has an easy job picking it up. When you are checking out where the eye of the needle is in relation to the shuttle hook you will find that the shuttle race will be in the way if you haven't followed directions and are trying out your super vision.. You can see the bottom half of the shuttle but not the hook. When you are happy you understand how your machine is operating, remove the bobbin and bobbin case, unattach the shuttle casing while keeping your finger on the shuttle. Don't let it move! The little prick looking thing sticking out that the bobbin and bobbin case were stuck on is attached to the shuttle hook. Hold it in place. Slowly, slowly, slowly rotate the hand wheel. Now you will see the shuttle in all its glory. You will see how it could pick up the thread, if you hadn't dismantled half the equipment! But most importantly you can measure the relationship between the needle and the shuttle.

The shuttle itself almost never gets out of whack. After all it just sits there going around in half circles. It doesn't have to pierce heavy cloth. It doesn't have to drag a heavy sail across the Machine. But if you do have to adjust it, follow the lower drive shaft under the machine. Don't be fooled by the keeper rings. The adjustment you want is just needle side of the cam at the end of the shaft. Very little adjustments make for big changes. Be sure to scribe the position you started at before loosening anything. (By scribing I mean drawing or scratching a continuous line on the shaft and the cam so later you can match up the lines to return to where you started or measure how much you have adjusted.) As always in adjusting cams, great care must be taken. You can really screw up by adjusting cams. Best thing to do is take a series of digital photos as you go along to be able to always return to the start. Stop freaking out! You will never have to time a shuttle hook. In over 300 sewing machines I have timed, I had to adjust the shuttle hook once. Repeat, just once. I would draw you a picture of how to adjust the shuttle, but then you would do it and screw up your machine. If you really, really think it is your shuttle, come find me, I'll adjust it for free. (If you bought the book!) (Hee, hee, hee!) (Hey! I made a rhyme!)

Measure the distance above the point of the needle that the point of the shuttle hook (the top and middle of the three shuttle hooks) is, just as the shuttle hook's tip is at the beginning to touch the shaft of the needle. The tip of the hook should be between one and three cds above the tip of the needle. If it isn't adjust the depth the needle projects past the shuttle.

To adjust the depth of the needle depends on the machine. Almost always, you will be using a design based on a Singer copyright. Really. Singer invented modern day sailing. If it wasn't for Singer only millionaires would be sailing around the world! Because they don't have to repair their own sails. In the Singer design, the needle shaft is timed by a set screw which holds the shaft at various heights above the base plate. The base plate is the flat part of the Machine where the material passes across when it is being sewn. Below the base plate is the Black Hole of Calcutta. If your needle is incorrectly timed, if the shuttle hook is not 3/32" above the point of the needle after the needle (and needle shaft) have been raised 3/32", if not then release the set screw and realign the depth that the needle (and needle shaft) project. Measure the distance the needle has raised when the shuttle hook just touches the side of the needle. Actually the hook doesn't touch the needle, the needle goes in the valley inside of the hook, but pretend that the hook does touch the needle, and measure that way.

It really isn't hard. Hold in place the little prick looking thing that sticks out and is attached to the shuttle hook after you release the shuttle race and remove the race, bobbin and bobbin case; turn the hand wheel till the shuttle hook is just preparing to touch the beginning of the needle, measure the distance the needle has raised at this point from its bottom most point. What could be easier?

What? You are still confused?

The shuttle hook can't pick up the top thread if the needle is going down or is down because the top thread is still tight to the needle. It is only after the needle starts to go up that a loop starts to form. The loop is at its biggest when the needle has raised between 1/32" and 3/32" from its bottom most point. The Machine is doing other things at the same time, it is getting ready to advance the material with the presser foot, it is getting ready to pull the loop out of the top thread and pull the top thread the rest of the way around the bobbin case with the take up arm, but all of that is tied in to the movement of the needle bar. As long as we time the needle bar and shuttle hook correctly the Machine will work well. Everyone has to pull together at the end, but they can't pull and make a knot if the shuttle hook hasn't picked up the top thread! All you have to do is adjust the needle so the shuttle hook and the needle can have a nice little date, 50 times a second!

Timing the Needle and Shuttle Hook

For Sail-Rite and other Commercial Machines

As machines get bigger and more powerful, the designers didn't believe, quite rightly, a little crimp screw would hold the needle shaft in place. The older sailrites are of these designs. The newer ones have a set screw much like domestic machines. (Bummer, huh?) The ones that don't, have an access hole on the back of the needle arm case. Remove the cover and twirl the hand wheel this way and that. (It is OK to move the hand wheel either way without thread in the machine. Never turn the wheel's top away from you when it is threaded.) The access hole leads to a set screw on a cam in the back. Just to be mean hearted, it is designed to be adjusted when the needle is not in its lowest position.

If your machine's timing is out, ease off the set screw slightly, return the needle to its lowest position, then twist the hand wheel while holding the needle arm stationary, till it is correct as in the last chapter. You may have to ease off the set screw several times till the shuttle and needle will move independently, but, please, don't ease it off too far. Are you starting to realize why they pay sewing machine repairmen such big bucks?

Before you get started, check your needle. Sailrites and all commercial machines use longer needles than domestic machines. Hopefully, which needle is required is included in your machine's documentation. If not look on the internet. Failing that, most Notions stores will have a wide variety of needles for sale, all with descriptions on the back of the package for which machines they are designed for. (Sister Ann Margaret hit me with a ruler across the knuckles each time I ended a sentence with a preposition. Isn't it fun being grown up and all? Such Freedom!)

Adjusting the Feed Dog and Presser Foot

OK, the needle and shuttle hook are now timed. (If not, go back and read the above one sentence at a time until you finally get it. No shame. This is fairly difficult to grasp at first.) But another thing (Yes, another) can go wrong. The material being sewn has to be brought forward. (or back depending on how you are looking at it!). Two things have to be adjusted here. The height the jaws of the feed dog come up out of the black hole of Calcutta, and also the force the presser foot holds the material against the feed dog.

Adjusting the Presser Foot

The presser foot is lifted by means of a lever on the back side of the Machine. NEVER, never operate the Machine with the presser foot in the raised position. When the needle is going up, when it is withdrawing itself from the material, the presser foot is holding down the material. If it didn't, if the material is allowed to lift, no stitch can be made. The material, needle and top thread will lift away from the shuttle hook and the hook will not be able to grab the loop of top thread, and a missed stitch will occur.

To fix this you must increase pressure on the presser foot. First, test to see if the foot is raising. With the needle in the material (you want to be sure to keep fingers away from the pointy end of the needle at all times, if the needle hits your finger, it will bend the needle, and also it really hurts), with the needle in the material put your finger on part of the presser foot and turn the hand wheel to go through an entire cycle, that is make a stitch. If you can feel the presser foot being pulled up by the needle you have to dial in more pressure on the presser foot. This is done by pushing down on the plunger on the top of the Machine just above of the needle bar inspection port. Keep pushing down the plunger till the presser foot doesn't "bounce" when the needle comes up. If you push too far, press down on the ring around the plunger and the plunger will jump up to a minimal pressure setting. In some Machines you twist the top knob, to the right or clockwise to increase pressure or to the left or anti-clockwise to decrease pressure.

The heavier the material the greater the pressure has to be on the presser foot. New sailcloth requires especially strong pressure. It may be on your domestic Machine that the spring that holds down the presser foot is inadequate for heavy sailcloth. In that case a stronger spring can be installed by easing the set screw just below the pressure release ring and

46

unscrewing the lock nut, removing the old spring, installing the new, tighten the lock nut and the set screw. Sewing machine stores have a wide variety of springs in different strengths.

Adjusting the Feed Dog

The feed dog lives down in the black hole of Calcutta and is responsible for bringing the material forward when the needle has been withdrawn from the black hole. The feed dog never gets out of timing as there is little force on it to make it do so. However, we can adjust how far the teeth of the feed dogs come out of the needle plate. The heavier and stiffer (like sailcloth) material requires the teeth to come all the way up. This is so important that commercial sailmaking Machines have a walking foot which forwards the material in a more dependable manner. However for us, with our little Machines, if we need to sew heavier material, sometimes we have to help the feed dog along as we guide the material to be sewn to the needle.

To adjust the height that the teeth of the presser foot project through the needle plate, raise the Machine up and look underneath the Machine or remove the face plate and look in from the back of the Machine. Go ahead and play with the lever you find there. (I know it has teeth but I promise it won't bite.) At the low setting the teeth don't even project through the plates. In this case you would have to move the material being sewn yourself, a good way to break or bend a needle if you are not very comfortable with sewing. Adjusted properly, your feed dog teeth will make your life a lot easier. If the material bunches up between stitches, lower the teeth and decrease bottom thread tension. What could be easier?

That is it! You did it! You timed your very own sewing machine! People are going to listen to you at cocktail parties, not that E. F. Hutton guy. He never timed any sewing machines. Congratulations!

Advanced Tricky Operating Tips

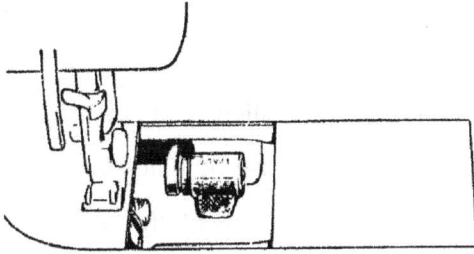

The number one complaint of every sailmaker is they can't get enough top tension. They twist the friction plates as tight as they will go, the loosen off the bottom tension as much as they can and still the top of the sail looks fine but the bottom is a mass of loops and knots and it looks terrible and how can I put this sail up in the air where everyone can see it and they will all laugh at me and I will just die of shame and it is all that stupid top tensions fault.

Yes, it is. But come on, girl/guy. If you need more tension, add more tension. Really! No, that isn't a stupid statement. You don't have to rely on silly little friction plates when sewing sails that could repel bullets! How? Easy. Lead the thread coming from your spool or cone through a maze of friction creating objects before leading it back down to your machine and its little friction plates. For example, lead the thread up to a book shelf and loop the thread around the book retaining bar as many times as is needed. Generally, twist the line around a half inch piece of doweling twice for each ounce weight of material you are trying to sew. If you are on deck, twist the thread around a mast step. If you are ashore, loop the thread around a tree limb or an exposed piece of wiring. Be inventive. If you need top tension, add friction.

Experienced sailmakers rarely take on big jobs without securing the seams first with double sided sticky tape. This insures that the sail is made correctly and quickly. The problem arises that the needle eventually becomes slightly sticky from the tape and the thread tends to stick to the needle instead of forming a loop for the shuttle hook. To prevent this Everytime you change the bobbin just wipe the needle with a slightly oily cloth or even better an anti-static wipe used in clothes dryers. Make it a habit.

Conclusion

I could not imaging going cruising without a sewing machine. Compared to the price of sails, they are incredibly cheap. Just for the price of one new jib, you could buy one or two new machines and for an used jib, 3 or 4 used machines.

If you just sit around making bed sheets or dresses, you would never have to time your machine. But, we sailors don't. We make our little domestic machines sew through 8 or 10 layers of the strongest cloth ever invented! They use Kevlar to make bullet proof vests and we make our machines sew through it! It is little wonder, after all that mechanical torture, they might need a little TLC. TLC for a sewing machine is cleaning and keeping it timed.

Would you run your diesel with only 2 of 4 injectors firing? Would you run your windless if it missed every other link? Don't abuse your sewing machine. If you take care of it, it will survive longer than your boat, make beautiful repairs, and even make new awnings and sails.

I hope this book will encourage you to buy a sewing machine if you don't already have one and to use your machine, if you have one, instead of sending work out to the sailmakers and to take one more step in being independent of civilization. One day you might sail around the world in joy and laughter secure in the knowledge that storms may rip your sails, but you can sew them right back up again.

Your westward bound forbearers are going to be very proud of you. Well done!